CW00544304

FINDING ME

Published under licence by Brown Dog Books and The Self-Publishing
Partnership Ltd, 10b Greenway Farm, Bath Rd, Wick, nr. Bath BS30 5RL

www.selfpublishingpartnership.co.uk

ISBN printed book: 978-1-83952-482-0
ISBN e-book: 978-1-83952-483-7

Cover design by Kevin Rylands
Internal design by Andrew Easton

Printed and bound in the UK

This book is printed on FSC certified paper

FINDING ME

A journey of discovery that has set me free from the emotional bonds and beliefs of the past.

A W MILLS

BROWN DOG BOOKS

*To free myself from my emotional bonds and
beliefs of the past
by rewriting my life script*

A few words from a hero of mine before we start

The content and purpose of *Finding Me* was succinctly put by Billy Connolly in his autobiography *Windswept and Interesting*, when he said, 'A baby has no means of defence at all. It relies a hundred percent on you. You have to just love it. That's the only answer. Some people make a separate room for it and let it cry until it stops – until it's lost the will to appeal to you. Let it be, let it climb all over you and feel that you're always there to save it, because it thinks it's in danger. Afraid of dying. Just let it be.' (Two Roads 2021 p247)

Contents

Finding me   9

In the beginning   12

Early years   16

Primary school   19

Secondary school   24

Adolescence   29

Reflection on my formative years   34

Become a man, son   38

Down the pub   40

Relationships and marriage   45

Alcoholics Anonymous and the start of my recovery journey   49

New beginning   53

The beginning of the end   58

Endgame   62

Getting off the wheel of life   65

Life script   69

My life script   77

Quietening my inner child   84

The new life script   87

Writing your new life script   93

Other actions that I have taken   98

A note to the reader   99

In the end I was never really alone   100

Bibliography   101

Finding me

My life story is one of hope. It is my struggle to find a love of self and a freedom from my own belief system. It is about success in the face of perceived adversity. It is about finding me.

I am now fast approaching my sixty-sixth birthday but it is only in the last five years that I have started to live the life that I always wanted to live. To be the person that I have always wanted to be. Prior to this I was a prisoner of my own self belief system and I had gone through life repeating the same behaviours over and over again. Despite everything that I achieved there was always that belief, that I was not good enough and that I was not wanted. These twin beliefs were the bars of a cell that kept me a prisoner for the majority of my life.

If like me you live with the fear of not being good enough or of not being wanted and you want to find freedom by changing your life, you can! It is possible to learn to love yourself and to come to believe that you have the power to change and achieve this. If you can follow the simple suggestions that are within these pages and you have the courage to seek your true self then this book is for you. It will empower you to find your true self.

Your journey hopefully will not take you as long as mine and almost certainly it will be different to mine. You may have caused less damage and upset than me and hopefully you avoided the illness of addiction. If, however, whatever your life circumstances may be, at your core, you feel less than and unwanted, then you are a fellow traveller on the same road that I trudged for so many years.

My belief is simple – we are the product of our upbringing and our experiences in childhood define who we are. They drive our emotional state and our behaviours; we may try to hide them as best as we can but we can't entirely and eventually they will create a repeating pattern of behaviours and experiences that define who we are.

This need not be the case. Every child that is conceived and born is precious and should be loved and nurtured so that they can develop into a rounded, loving human being. Unfortunately our parents or care givers can only parent with the skills they have and with the experience of the way they were parented: the way that they interact with us is driven by their own belief systems and experiences. Therefore, if a young child doesn't feel loved or secure, due to its parents' own experiences and emotional needs, it will become detached from its parents' love and have begun to seek ways to fill that gaping hole of emptiness that it feels inside.

As we grow and begin to form relationships and live our lives, the frightened child continues to cry out for love and security, or runs away from anything that feels frightening. No matter how well we try to suppress it the fear of not being good enough, of not being loved, will be clearly demonstrated in our character in some way. Those suppressed feelings will be the key drivers that keep us prisoners of our own low self-will and low self-esteem; our own self-loathing. These patterns repeat themselves again and again as we grow older and become more and more embedded in these behaviours. Over time new fear-based coping skills in hiding our fears will be sought out and found as we struggle to live life on life's terms.

This is called by many the 'inner child'. While you may be an adult and married with a career and a family, your emotional responses and behaviours are still driven by that frightened child inside you. Reacting by flailing and thrashing around inside yourself, desperately looking for love but never really believing that you deserve it or will find it. Good relationships may be subconsciously sabotaged. Good people pushed away.

The belief system that we create and the behaviours it drives have come to be called our 'life script'. We were given it as an infant, practised it as a child and by the age of seven or eight it was ingrained into us. A life script based not in love and security but in fear and isolation. Rehearsals will have been completed. Now we simply step onto the stage each day repeating and reliving a daily existence based on a script that we had no control over. If this is the case then deep-rooted pain is an inevitability. We will of course try to find comfort. However, in many ways what we thought gave us comfort actually just prolonged and deepened the pain of life.

What you will read below is my journey through life and how eventually after much searching I was to find peace and contentment, simply by learning to rewrite my own life script. A script based in love not fear. I invite you to read and to discover a better way, a way based on the truth of you today and not on the beliefs of that frightened child.

In the beginning

There is a black and white photograph that was taken of my brother and me sitting side by side on a white cupboard, with me holding the ear of a teddy bear. Looking at that picture now and seeing what looked like two happy children it is hard to believe the pain and darkness that was to engulf me for most of my life.

I was born in 1956 to parents who loved each other but who were already living the lives that their upbringing had created. My mum was born into poverty in a West London tenement block. Her parents were both very heavy drinkers and a regular chore for her was to take a pair of best and never-used sheets to the pawn shop every Monday to exchange for money to buy alcohol and food, only to return on Friday when her father got paid to reclaim the precious commodity. This process was repeated every week as the family, mainly due to alcohol, lived a hand-to-mouth existence.

As a child I used to visit mum's old home with my brother and mother. It was a sad, dark place, with little love and no real signs of a family life ever having existed there. It is best summed up by stories my mother tells of sitting outside pubs at night and of her long hair being cut and sold to wigmakers to buy drink. Her only respite was evacuation when she left home for several years to live in a lovely village outside London. It was idyllic and I have often wondered how my mother's life would have differed if she had stayed in that loving community; instead she came home to the stark realities and hardships of home life in London.

My dad tells a story that paints a picture of a thousand words. He told me that the first time mum ever received a Christmas present was when she visited my dad's family home on Christmas day. At the time she was in her early twenties and her belief systems and emotional nature were well embedded by then. She was overwhelmed to be given such a small gift. It went against everything that she had previously known. There was little love in her life, therefore she never expected love, felt loved and never loved herself. This is the tragedy that many suffer. As children we do not ask for, but are given through our parents and carers, the behaviours and emotions that mould us into the people we become. We are given a life script. Not one of our own but one created by those who were meant to care for and nurture us.

My dad also grew up in West London in a more loving family, where my happiest memories of childhood visits were listening to *Family Favourites* playing on the radio and the lovely smell of a Sunday roast that drifted throughout the house. Nan was a wonderful, strong, snuggly person, who had lived a hard life. Her hands used to shake, which was evidently due to her making and sleeping on bombs that she made during the First World War, while my Granddad, who won the Military Medal during the First War, was more distant. My strongest memory of him is that when he retired he sat down in his chair and said, 'I have done my bit, now I will rest,' and he did. For the rest of his life my memories of him are smoking rollups and sitting in his favourite chair.

My dad's upbringing and the impact of war on his parents created what I have always called the 'post-Victorian parent'. In his own way he was not cold or unloving but believed that boys should not cry. If you were hit, hit back. Stand up and fight for yourself; be a man, even when you are only ten years old. He was a practical man, a carpenter who believed that any problem could be solved by talking through it, and that eventually you would get over it. Life was difficult for me because while I looked like a boy, played like a boy and was big and strong, inside I always felt alone and scared and could never be what I then thought he wanted me to be.

My mum, on the other hand, was a very needy and emotional person who found life hard to deal with and has spent most of her life living with anxiety and depression. It was not her fault that was who she had grown up to believe she was. Both of them creations of their own upbringing and belief systems. Both playing the roles that they had been given and that they had learned to live by. Both in their own way in need of each other, like two damaged halves of a jigsaw piece, who when they found each other fitted together into one dysfunctional piece. My mother was very needy, full of feelings of low worth and low self-esteem, while my dad was emotionally closed down. A fixer in control of his emotions who believed that if only we all thought like him our emotional difficulties would disappear. Mum needed dad as much as dad needed mum, and into this they brought a new life, me!

I want to make it very clear that my parents loved me and did their very best, but they parented me based on the roles that they had learned to play in life and with the belief systems that they had developed over years of practice. In time even those around them came to believe this as well and consequently treated them in that same way. A never-ending, repeating journey of enforcing that which they came to believe was true, but in fact was and is the lie of them.

This idea of developed and enforced belief systems is at the heart of human emotional disturbance. A small child learns by watching, listening to and responding to its parents or care givers. This is fine if the modelling demonstrates love and emotional security. Parents, however, no matter how much they love their children, only have the tools and beliefs that they hold, based on their own life experiences which they then model to their offspring. Therefore it is clear that we learn from our parents and caregivers. So if the parents have emotional difficulties that is all they have to share with their children. The negative cycle continues as their own negative life script is passed on to their child. To never know the truth of who you are meant to be, and to never live a life free from fear is, I believe, the biggest crime any parent, however unwittingly, can bequest to their offspring.

Early years

I was born in 1956, the first child to my parents. Conceived in love, to grow and develop in the security of my mother's womb until birth. I have come to believe that there is little learning achieved in the womb apart from that of survival. What we do learn or what affects us is the consequences of the actions and behaviours of the mother. A calm and healthy mother has more chance of delivering a calm and healthy child, rather than one who is over emotional or who makes bad choices.

What a baby needs is warmth and care to meet its needs but most importantly it needs security and love. To know by its parents' actions that it is wanted and loved. To be spoken to in a loving way and as time passes to be praised and rewarded for its efforts. To be aware of the loving boundaries set up and practised by its parents. In short, for a baby to become a happy toddler it needs to feel secure, safe and loved.

I do not ever remember feeling like this. I always felt outside and unloved. I am not aware of when this started but it is the damaged rock on which my life's script was built. A script learnt by observing the emotions and behaviours of my parents. I think my mum's inability to give love unconditionally due to her upbringing and life experiences played a part, as did my father's lack of emotional literacy. My understanding is that I was left to cry, not picked up when upset, not cuddled, not made to feel safe and secure. This was not to punish me, this is what they believed was right.

The outcome was inevitable. I grew up feeling unloved by my mum while constantly trying to please my dad. To be whom I believed he wanted me to be. Boys don't cry. But I did! Boys can stand up for themselves. I couldn't! Boys are strong, unemotional. I wasn't. These beliefs were as untrue then as they are now, but how they manifested themselves left me feeling alone, isolated and scared. This situation was not helped when eighteen months after my birth, my little brother was born. I believe that this badly affected me, because quite naturally he needed more care and time and as I was older, I could be left alone to play.

Many years later when I attended an Inner Child group it was explained to me that when you are born the reason you are placed on your mother's chest is to start the bonding process, which future loving acts would then enforce. I seem to have not received this connection and bonding and to this day I do not feel it. If your mum fails to make you feel safe and secure, your dad is the backup who can step in to support his wife. My dad could not do that, he was too emotionally closed down; everything for him was logical, a problem to be solved.

If you do not receive this early bonding from your parents, you are not connected to love. You are unplugged and flail around in the darkness, afraid and lost, screaming and lashing out in fear. In the process of doing this you learn over time about attention-seeking behaviours – how to create a scene or situation. Run away, self-harm, do anything that will get you attention, because that is what is craved and that is what I never had. I was alone and unloved. It is interesting that my brother who is eighteen months younger than me and my sister who is twelve years younger than me are more like my dad. I think that they looked and learnt from me and chose a different way to get attention and feel loved. They are both quite arrogant and think they know best and have always seemed to look down on me, although that is at least partly due to my belief that they are loved more than me.

Primary school

At five years old I began my formal education at the local Primary School. My first teacher in the Infants class was lovely and I can still picture her reading to us at the end of the school day. The classroom was a treasure chest of adventures for young minds. We had a shop, a sand pit, bikes, a slide and colour everywhere! We even had a rabbit as a class pet. I remember very little about my time in the Infant school, which suggests that it was a happy time. This is because my memory is like a sieve, good memories slip through it, hardly leaving a mark behind, while bad memories stick and are hard to remove. During this time we also moved to our new home which was nearer to the school. It was in fact just a short walk to school, up an alleyway with trees on one side and a meandering brook on the other.

When I was seven I moved up into the Junior School and was placed in the 'A' stream. I do not remember it as a happy year, which is probably why I struggled and came low down in the class rankings. I just believed that I could not do it and basically I became an invisible child. It was also at this time that I started masturbating, both at home and at school. At home every night and whenever I felt the need in school. I used to go to the boys' toilets, shut myself in a cubicle and for those few short moments I felt better, it relieved my emotional pain. It has always surprised me that despite clear evidence of my nocturnal activities at home, neither of my parents ever said a word to me. There were clear boundaries about bedtimes and not leaving the table at mealtimes, but nothing to help me develop a balanced mental health outlook.

I do not remember really ever feeling emotionally safe. Looking back it was like I was in the dark, others seemed to be okay and part of a family while I always felt alone and unloved. I remember the end of year parents' evening that year, it was the only year that I remember my dad getting mad at me. He was angry because he did not understand why I did not try. I was in fact unknowingly enforcing the life script that had already been written for me – 'I am a failure, I can't do it, and I am unloved'. There were holidays and other happy times but they were like moments that drifted by. They were on the outside of me. My inner self was in charge. The die was cast. Insecure and frightened, believing that I was unloved and that emotional pain was normal.

There was an incident during this time that has never left me. There was a lad in school and he was one of those boys who would tease me for being an outsider. One day I lost my temper with him, it was like being possessed. I grabbed him by the hair and repeatedly banged his head against the school building until a teacher pulled me off him. I remember the hair and blood in my hand. The anger inside me had escaped and I had vented it on this boy. It marked me because I have ever since always avoided violence against others. I used to say it was because I was afraid of being hurt but the truth was that I was afraid of the damage I could do to somebody and, on some level, that I would enjoy it.

In subsequent years I remained in the second set and I was blessed with three teachers who could hold me emotionally. For the first time I understood emotional boundaries and I trusted and felt safe with them. They were all hard but fair. What made them important to me was the consistency they demonstrated throughout the year. I knew exactly where I stood and what was expected of me. They had no favourites and each of them was well known for their discipline and fairness.

In Year Two I won the merit award for progress, but while others around me were moved up I stayed where I was and, while very upset at the time, I now see that they were right. The lesson pace was slower, we used more concrete operations and visual examples which helped me to believe in myself a little more, and all three teachers set very clear and consistent boundaries. I also had sport which helped me to feel that I belonged, at least during the matches. I represented the school at football, cricket and athletics, winning the district sports for the obstacle race. These achievements were later badly tarnished by the achievements of my brother, who was a better footballer and faster runner. It seemed that whatever I did he did better, which in my eyes completely devalued my achievements.

In Year Four I took the Eleven Plus and was a border case for Grammar School. The headmaster told my dad that he did not think that I was Grammar School material due to my sensitive nature. At this time I was also worried about other boys in my year who I believed did not like me. However, the more likely truth is that I isolated myself from them, did not join in games with them and was easily upset. I had become what I feared most – unloved and alone. The pattern was set and kept on repeating itself. I moved towards and became what I thought about. I believed that I was alone and unloved and that is what I created, and others came to expect that of me.

I did not want to go with the local boys to the local secondary school. I wanted to get away from them and have a fresh start. My dad wanted me to go to a practical school so that I could develop my woodwork skills, as that is what he wanted me to be, because that is what he was. The secondary school that he chose was also a very sporty school and had won many awards. Therefore it was decided to give me a fresh start at a school my dad thought would be good for me. I was offered and accepted a place at a secondary school five miles from home. On my last day in primary school we lined up to shake the headmaster's hand and say goodbye. While others were happy, I cried and was inconsolable. It was not leaving the school that hurt, it was leaving the teachers that made me feel safe. My insides cried out but nobody could hear, and I believed nobody would be listening.

Before going on, I think it is worth stating how I perceived the achievements of my younger brother and sister and how their later success impacted on me. Academically on leaving primary school both my brother and sister achieved more than me. On leaving primary school my brother won a free place at the local Grammar School and my sister finished high up academically and went on to be placed in the highest sets for all her subjects at secondary school. My brother and sister were better athletes than me and my brother was a better footballer than me. Even when passing our cycling proficiency tests they did better than me. I scored 98, my brother scored 99 and my sister scored 100.

Most importantly they were liked and had lots of friends, while I did not. To my mind it seemed that they were better than me, something my brother teased me about a lot. He would say something nasty, I would get upset and chase him. He would run indoors to mum or dad and get there before I could catch him. I would get told off for trying to hurt him and he would quietly walk away, leaving me feeling that yet again I had not been treated fairly. All these years later they still have the power, if I let them, to hurt me and despite my best efforts to love, help and support them, their actions towards me mean that for now the best that I can do for my peace of mind is to stay away from them. This is yet another consequence of a dysfunctional family because, in their own ways, both my brother and sister were affected in ways that dictated their actions and subsequent lifestyle choices.

Secondary school

A good summary of my secondary school years is best summed up by my father who, many years later, made a comment that demonstrates the imprint and pain that my experiences at that school left on him. While I was working the Alcohol Anonymous 12-step program or recovery and doing my amends to my dad for the harms that I had caused him, he held his hand up to stop me talking, looked at me and said that he owed me an amend as well. I was puzzled. 'What for?' I asked him. 'For sending you to that school,' he said. 'It was the biggest mistake that I ever made with one of my children. It was wrong and I am sorry.' Hindsight is a wonderful thing but at the time both of us thought it was the right school for me. How wrong we were.

My secondary school was a very large all-boys' school. It took me two buses to get there and there was only one boy from my primary school who went with me. This was a totally new environment and not one suited to an emotional young lad. The area was also different, it was more working class and the nature of the boys there reflected that. It was impossible not to feel and to be treated differently from others. I always saw the gentler side of things. I was scared of war and afraid of violence, while most boys around me seemed at ease with both.

There seemed to be no nurturing teachers, like those who had supported me previously. The playground with 500 boys in it felt like a battleground and it was no place to tell others that I liked *Little House on the Prairie* and cried at sad things. My behaviours and emotional nature singled me out and I was labelled a cry-baby and gay. I became the subject of much teasing and the victim of many practical jokes. Needless to say, with the exception of sport I did not do very well academically. I could never understand why the camaraderie of a football or rugby team disappeared from those same boys when they became part of a bigger group in and around school. It was much later in Alcoholics Anonymous that I came to understand the power of group dynamics and the power that those within the group had over those few who were on the outside. It is the same as the safety achieved by belonging to any group, whereby everybody who is inside the group acts and thinks the same and those who do not are outsiders. I was that outsider: I was different. While they were secure with each other, I had no one!

The other problem was that at that time the different groups of youths from the different towns were fighting each other. As I went to school in a different town I was harassed by the boys where I lived and by those who came from another town and went to my secondary school. It was hard to go anywhere and feel safe, so I stayed in my bedroom listening to Status Quo and Rod Stewart played very loudly to drown out the thoughts and feelings that I had. There was no safety at school and no safety out and about. What had I done that was so wrong, to be treated and to feel this way?

It was during these years that I developed several activities to change how I felt. Apart from masturbating, I would use a needle and cotton and thread it under the skin on my feet and hands and then rip it out. The sensation of tearing changed momentarily how I felt. I also took to swallowing cotton because when it came out, I used to love the feeling of pulling it through me; again, it changed how I felt. By then I had also started hitting things and banging my head against a wall. My parents' answer to my obvious distress was my dad telling me that I had to stand up for myself and to not be afraid, while the heightened anxiety between my mum and me just reduced our relationship to one of shouting at each other, with me blaming her for everything. She used to say, 'I don't know what to do with you', and get very upset. She was lost, I was lost, - what hope was there?

I remember one day writing a note saying that I was running away and that it was her fault. I then hid in a tree and watched, enjoying her suffering as she searched for me. I had learned attention seeking and emotional blackmail. I wanted to hurt her, to make her suffer, just like she had hurt me. I was repeating what I had learnt as a toddler and my dad was the enabler. I did not have a chance and they were doing their best with the tools they had. The cycle continued.

Two other things happened at this time that were to impact greatly on me. When I was twelve my mum gave birth to my little sister. Later I learnt that people have children to fix problems. I do not know if this was why my sister was conceived but what I do know is that it had the opposite effect. At the time my mum was in her mid-thirties, and somebody locally told her she was too old to have a baby and that it was dirty. The effect on my mum was tumultuous, it opened old wounds and her mental health deteriorated. I remember a psychiatrist coming to see her and telling dad that the trauma was due to her childhood experiences and the subsequent feelings and beliefs that she held and believed about herself. There was no real understanding then of PTSD, the answer was Valium, which my mum for a while became dependent on. She also took to her bed and could not get up. In fact, she stayed indoors for several years. A lot of the baby's care fell on me and dad. I used to wash and change her and play with her. I thought by loving and caring for her, my mum would love and care for me. It did not happen that way; nothing changed. In fact, my sister grew up following the same pathway as my brother. Both were emotionally distant and seemed immune to the feelings that I had. At the same time I felt even more abandoned, now I was third in importance. There was no sunlight on the horizon. I clearly remember that hollow feeling of emptiness and loss.

This was when fear took a greater and more corrosive grip on my life. I had a powerful imagination and in a mind full of loneliness and sadness, it now seems obvious that I would be drawn to thinking about death. I used to wake at night screaming and petrified of dying and the nothingness that followed. My mind would see things creeping out of walls, dead people coming to get me. My mind used to try and work out where the end of the universe was and what life was about. To my mind this was horrendous and I suffered what I can only describe as living nightmares. I used to run downstairs desperate to escape, and my dad would be there to tell me it was just a dream and that it would be alright. Of course, it never was. I used to do anything to try and think of something else or feel something else, most of which I have described earlier. The truth, however, was it just put off the inevitable, the night terrors were coming regardless. I was in my mid-teens when I was taken to see our doctor and he prescribed Valium to help me cope.

Life continued to be very difficult at school and I remember that we built canoes and took them camping overnight. I had to be driven home in the early hours of the morning because I panicked and became unwell when I saw the lights of cars on the road across the lake. I believed it was the dead people coming for me. As you can imagine, this did not do my street credibility in school much good and 'scaredy baby' became a chant I heard often.

It was at this point that I thought I had found a solution to my problems. I had a sexual encounter with a young man on a riverbank, which to be honest I quite enjoyed. Somebody was paying attention to me and it was demonstrated by a sexual act. This was the answer – sex meant love and I was gay. It fitted, I was emotional, scared of violence, I cried at sad films. I was either gay or I was in the wrong body and should have been a girl. These two questions played on my mind for a long time. I kept asking myself, was I gay or was I a woman in the wrong body? Clearly I was effeminate. The problem was, who could I ask or talk to? Not my parents or teachers and definitely not the boys in school. It was my secret and I kept that secret alone, frightened and confused by who or what I really was.

It is hard to describe how I felt at this time. The simplest way of putting it is that there seemed no hope. This was my life. My head teacher and dad decided that it would be best if I left school early and worked with my dad. That I needed my family around me. To the outside world they were right but in truth what they suggested just placed me right at the centre of the problem.

Adolescence

There is a truth in the saying; 'if nothing changes, nothing changes', and this is true for the next period of my life. My personal belief system and behaviour patterns were by now well embedded and drove my daily life, constantly enforcing the internal messages, that I was 'less than' and 'nobody loves me' mantra.

At home nothing much changed; if anything it got worse. My relationship with my mum and me blaming her for how I felt continued, with my dad having long talks with both of us and even putting us in a room together to 'sort things out'. The problem was there was only ever one set of messages running around and around in my head, with them saying, 'You don't love me' and my mum saying, 'I can't cope' and dad saying, 'Tell me what's wrong and we can sort it out'. I spent hours listening to loud music and struggled with nightmares and fears of death. I was still doing things to myself to change how I felt but in truth fear, depression, low self-esteem and anxiety were my constant companions. They were always there in the background deciding which one of them was going to come out to play next. The voices in my head never stopped: 'They don't love you, you can't do it, and you're not worth it.' Both my mother and I were regular visitors to the local doctor, who would listen and do his best, but to my recollection nothing changed. In my case he sent me to see a couple of people to try to help me, but all I did was to blame my mum, their best advice being to leave home when I was able.

I undertook several different jobs during this period but I could never settle and there was always a reason to leave. I started a carpentry apprenticeship but left because I could not cope with college as my anxieties made me feel constantly claustrophobic. I was a school caretaker but left because the head teacher messed up my nice clean hall floor and I was sure that he did it on purpose, just because he did not like me. Eventually at about seventeen years old things got so bad that I joined Community Service Volunteers and left home to work.

Prior to leaving home and despite my fears about my sexuality I had two girlfriends. I believed on both occasions that I was in love and that therefore they must love me; in truth we were all just starting out on the relationship journey and mine was based on the fear of abandonment that led to the need for me to control. In the end they both decided that I was not what they wanted and on both occasions I spent hours pleading on the phone, only in the end to have their parents contact mine to ask them to get me to desist. I can remember the feeling of abandonment that these brief romances caused and the uncontrollable negative emotions that followed. Like a baby, I threw the toys out of the pram and screamed the place down. I did manage to get some attention out of the situations, however, as I twice threatened to kill myself, which sent people running to me to make sure that I was safe. These were further opportunities to pour my emotional discontent out, over some well-meaning person.

Things would be okay now, I was leaving home to work and all my problems would be left behind me. I was sent to a respite home for children in Norfolk. I arrived, unpacked, got scared and rang my dad to come and get me. I think for the first time he did the right thing – he said, 'No'. He told me that I could do it if I tried and that it would be good for me. Through running tears and a snotty nose, I agreed and did something for the first time that on reflection would have been better not to do. I went and got four cans of beer. The next morning things did not seem so bad and I met the children in the home. There were kids there with a wide variety of difficulties including thalidomide, emotional difficulties and physical difficulties. Very quickly I began to enjoy this role, I felt needed and the kids seemed to like me. In particular there were three brothers who all had emotional and behavioural problems. They were great. In fact I was just like them and we got on like a house on fire. Here was my tribe and a place where I could be part of something. At the end of the placement I asked if I could next go to a home that was entirely for children with emotional and behavioural problems. I understood them, I believed that I could help them. If I could make them okay then surely I would be okay.

I was sent to a residential home just outside Luton. It was a home for children who were beyond the support and care of their local authority. All the children had emotional and behavioural problems and all were from London and were on care orders. The house was split into three family groups and the staff lived in the attic. The whole place felt like home. People cared for each other and for the children and each group was a family. In truth it was chaos at times and the bad behaviour was not only from the children. One day three staff took a minibus into London with nine boys to visit the Natural

History Museum. We told the kids to go explore and went and found a bar. It took us ages to round up the kids, especially after a few drinks, and on the way back the side door of the minibus fell off and we had to lash it back on the side of the van to get us home. On another occasion we took everybody to see the film *Rollerball* and when we got back the kids wanted to play it in the gym, so we all donned cricket and hockey pads and went for it. As you can imagine, there were plenty of walking wounded the following day. We were as bad as the boys in many ways.

I loved working there, dealing with challenging children made me feel worthwhile, and I felt at home. The difficulty was I could not stop. I was always doing extra shifts and spent hours worrying about the children. By now I was drinking every evening, but as I always drank in a group it was kept under control. I remember one night that I walked to the local pub. I just wanted to be on my own and of course, once there I felt lonely so I got sadder and drunker. On the way back, I felt desolate and decided to beat myself up. I remember punching and head-butting a tree, scraping my face and arms on the road and tearing my shirt. When I got back to the home, I woke a staff member and said that I had been attacked. That got me attention and, like many other times, caused even greater problems for me. After telling the story several times I fell asleep but in the morning the police turned up to get a statement as the housemaster had rung them. I could not tell the truth so I talked about a group of youths on mopeds who jumped me. The police officer said that as far as he knew there was no local gang of kids on mopeds. I was convinced they knew that I was lying and the fear of being found out was far worse than any attention that I had gotten due to my lies.

In the end the inevitable happened, I could not leave the job alone. It was my job to fix these boys. I understood them. The problem was I gave all of my emotional energy away, which led to physical and emotional exhaustion setting in. Despite many attempts to help me I could not let go. It was like some kind of self-destruction. It did not matter what happened to me as long as the boys were okay. By saving them I could save myself. Finally, I had a nervous breakdown and was sent home.

Despite my effort to fix myself by fixing others nothing had changed, except that I felt more of an outsider after I had returned home. The rest of my family were still playing the same old roles and I was still the emotionally unstable one. My mum could not cope. My dad was the enabler and both my brother and sister had an arrogance about them and seemed to look down on me. Neither seemed to ever do anything wrong. I can remember mum saying, 'Look how well your brother and sister are doing, why you can't just be more like them?' I was the emotional runt of the pack, still feeling alone and still feeling unwanted.

Reflection on my formative years

It occurred to me while reflecting on my memories to date that according to what is written down there was very little to smile or laugh about in my childhood and teenage years. This of course would be untrue; however, happy memories can be hard to find. There are a few glimpses of something in a swirling mist but nothing with any substance. Suddenly you think you see something emerging into view and then just as quickly it is gone and all that is left is just a faint memory of an event. The other difficulty is that I have spent a lifetime feeding and enforcing my negative memories, putting together events that happen over time in my mind until it seems that there was no sunlight in between. No happy memories to draw on and no sense of a warm glow of remembrance.

While the beliefs about myself and my experiences were real and remained real in my mind for a long time, as time has gone by I have be able to look back on those formative years with the luxury of hindsight. I have come to understand that part of my difficulty in creating my memories is that my mind is like a sieve. Negative or bad experiences stick, while positive memories fall like sand through the holes and are much harder to hang onto.

For example, one of the happy times I remember is that

every year we went on a family holiday and I remember the sun shining, and swimming in the sea. My best memory is of holidays on the Isle of Wight. We used to rent a caravan and, while I do not remember the ferry crossings or most of what we did, I do remember the Horlicks and pasties that we got every evening just before we went to bed. We used to carry the mug with a pasty on a plate from the cafeteria back to the caravan and then sit down and consume our treat. I do not remember the taste or have any other memories of it. I just remember that we did it and I liked it. For some reason it stuck in the sieve. We also used to walk across the cliff tops to play pitch and putt golf, which was meant to be fun and which I always looked forward to. However, my memories of these games is of getting more and more frustrated with myself because I could not get the ball to go where I wanted. The more frustrated I got, the worse it got and the more my brother seemed to enjoy it. It's crazy that even when playing a little game of golf with my dad and brother, I was driven by my fear of failure and low self-esteem. So the happy memories were like sand and just slipped through my grasp. How could I have happy memories when my inner self cried out failure?

I continued playing sport throughout this period of my life, predominately football. It is true that I was selected for every team that I had trials with and that over the years I was part of different teams that won both cups and leagues. Surely this was something to remember positively, something to celebrate, but my memory of that time is that I was constantly worrying that I was not good enough and that I would be dropped for the next game. I used to wait for the team to be listed every week on the notice board, fully expecting my name not to be there, but every week it was. Why did I never learn that my place was secure? Why could I not except that I was good enough? Isn't that some kind of insanity? I never learnt that lesson and many years later, both at college and university, I was to repeat this behaviour by going to the marks office and challenging my results, not because they were too low, but because I did not believe that I was clever enough to do so well. My negative belief system was to strong, even when confronted by clear and concise evidence.

I also remember my despair when every year I finished second to another boy in school at the school sports, which everybody said was good because he was a county runner, only to have any happiness destroyed as my brother yet again won his event by yards. He was first. I was second, a failure in my eyes. Even though I was not even competing against my brother, my belief system took those two separate outcomes and decided I was a failure and my brother was better than me.

Finally there was the cycling proficiency test. When I was in year 4 at junior school, I scored 98%. 'Well done!' my parents cried, while I felt I should have scored 100%. At least, come the following year when my brother did the same test I should beat him. I remember him coming home and shouting at me, '99%, I won!'. Failed again. Then a few years later my younger sister did the same test. Surely I could beat a girl. 'Look, mum!' she cried. 'I scored 100%!'. What is interesting about this is that my brother just smiled and said that the test must have been easier, while I felt desperate he did not seem to care. Not second this time, but third. Failed again!

If there was one thing that I could change about those

years, it would be the ability to celebrate my own personal achievements and to not have placed so much emphasis on comparing myself to others, or of the expectations that I placed on myself that were never achievable. I spent years believing that I had failed, when in truth I had achieved a lot and had always done my best.

Become a man, son

Approaching my eighteenth birthday and living back at home, I went to work with my dad. God bless him, an enabler through and through. He was going to fix me. The problem was, nothing had changed. We all just carried on playing the same roles. I still spent most of my time in my bedroom, blasting out Rod Stewart or Status Quo music. Even now, mention *Maggie May* to my mum and you can see her shudder. Loud music blocked out my negative thoughts and got me through the day, then masturbating helped me get to sleep. Nothing changes if nothing changes! It was during this period that my dad started trying to find me something to do. He tried to get me into a hobby; as he was a carpenter he tried to inspire me with furniture and toy making. The problem was, all I saw was failure and could never accept compliments. He also tried bingo. He used to take me to a bingo hall in an attempt to occupy my mind. Needless to say, I was not inspired.

Then one night he hit on what he believed would be the answer. 'Come on,' he said. 'I am going to take you over to the Working Men's Club for a drink.' My dad took me into the club, saying, 'I am sure that this will help you to overcome your problems and then you will feel more like a man.' I remember that evening as if it was yesterday. We walked into the bar and he ordered me a pint of light and bitter. After a couple of drinks

I felt myself relax, I undid my top shirt button, rolled up my sleeves, leant against the bar, lifted my head and raised my voice. I was home. I had found my medicine. I had joined my tribe. When I drank I changed. Over the course of a few drinks I went from a quiet, withdrawn boy to a loud, sociable bloke who was a member of the tribe.

The problem was that like other things such as food, exercise and chocolate, if it made me feel good I wanted more of it. Too much food or chocolate made me sick. Too much exercise made me tired. However, too much alcohol literally turned me from Dr Jekyll to Mr Hyde. I became either very aggressive or very melancholy. I would either fight or flee. I never had any idea what would happen once I crossed that line. In truth the problems drink caused only ended if and when I passed out, fell asleep or ended up in hospital or on the phone to the Samaritans. I had truly found my tribe. I was an alcoholic!

Down the pub

A definition of insanity is somebody who does the same thing again and again, expecting a different result. This is the story of my drinking. I only ever went out for a pint, but once started it was hard to stop. I used to stumble home and pass out or collapse onto the bed, waking up the next day to the realisation that on arrival home the night before, something had happened. What would follow were apologies and requests for forgiveness and promises that whatever it was would never happen again and that I would drink less. These promises never lasted a day because that evening I was back at the bar, repeating the same pattern over and over again. This daily routine remained the same until I moved in with my future wife.

During this period there were many insane and horrible incidents that I could retell here but after the first few they all blur into one long, sad story. I will restrict myself to the ones of those I recall that demonstrate how alcohol and emotion mixed together impacted further on my life, and the resulting chaos it caused.

One night I had been out drinking with my drinking buddy and arrived home feeling sad and alone. The more I thought about it, the worse I felt. I needed some attention. My solution to this was to swallow all my Valium as well as my mum's supply. I then walked to my mate's house and woke him and his family up, telling them that I could not go on and that I wanted to die. Through flowing tears I explained what I had done and, as expected, I got the attention that I craved. His family were caught up in my attention-seeking, as were the paramedics and my parents, who were phoned and included in this piece of theatre. Theatre is what is was because I wanted attention and I had created the situation to achieve it. Not a suicide attempt, but a cry for attention and, as I was to realise later, a cry for help.

I ended up having my stomach pumped and was admitted to the psychiatric ward, where I told anybody who asked that this was my mum's fault. She did not love or want me. I was transferred to a specialist psychiatric hospital and placed on a ward. Again I told the same story regarding my mum, and treatment was discussed and offered. All I had to do was to sign myself into their care. At this time I was too afraid to face change and the pub was calling, so I left, telling them that I was going to stay with friends. Instead I went back home and then in the evening went to the pub. I had had my fill of attention and now I was going back to my daily insanity.

A few years later I was playing football for the local Working Men's Club. The team decided to go on holiday to a resort in Spain. I was invited. I was on the inside. As the departure date got closer, I became more anxious. I was afraid of flying. I was afraid of being away from home and my mum and dad. I didn't like the sun. Needless to say, the night before we flew out I was very drunk. I had a few more drinks on the plane, which only topped me up and then on arrival in this strange land we had a Sangria welcome party. I loved Sangria and by early that evening I was in a local bar drinking it by the jug. Then the switch happened, suddenly I was full of fear and anxiety. I tried to call my dad from a payphone and got so frustrated that I could not get through that I trashed the phone box. I eventually got back to the hotel in a terrible state of anxiety, crying and pleading to go home. I was petrified. I remember coming to in my bedroom with somebody there looking after me. I was taken to the local doctor, who gave me medication to calm me down. The holiday company booked me on the next scheduled flight home. The flight is a blur due to the amount of medication that I had taken. On arrival home I went to see my doctor. I told him how I had felt while I was away and how it was my mum's fault. That I could not cope and wanted to die. He arranged for me to go into another psychiatric treatment centre. I needed help but on arrival I panicked and needed to escape, so I ran away and went home to begin that same old routine. I wanted help but was too scared to face it, so the pattern just continued.

I also had this habit when I was drinking, of taking railway journeys. I would go out for a drink, get loud, be happy and then the switch would come and almost instantaneously I felt alone, unwanted and afraid. I had to run away. It was very rare for me to remember my journeys but on most occasions I would travel across London and get a train to Margate. I have no idea why I went to Margate. However, by the time I got there I had changed again and was sad and lonely, feeling like a lost child. I used to ring my dad, who would drive from home to Margate to fetch me. He always believed he could fix me but in truth, despite his love for me, he just enabled me. Throughout those years my relationship with my mother was very fraught. She did not love me. It was her fault. We tried to sort it out, my dad tried to sort it out. In truth she could not change and I did not know that I needed to change. I also did not trust her and was very angry with her.

This anger came out in several ways. I would punch holes in walls. Slam and smash doors. I damaged cars and people's houses. On a couple of occasions I tried to punch my way through the brick bedroom wall to get to her but only ever hurt my hands. Just like a small child, I would lose control of my temper if I felt emotionally upset. The mist would come down and I would lash out just like a child. While a baby throws toys out of a pram or cot when upset, I smashed things. I was a full grown man but inside my younger self, my inner child was lashing out due to fear of not being loved and of feeling abandoned.

It is only by luck that I did not hurt anybody, because if this happened when I was out drinking I had no control over my anger whatsoever. I used to pick people up and throw them across the room, while growling and screaming at them like an animal. I think my experience regarding my anger as a child stopped me from hitting people, although there was a part of me that was always afraid of being hurt. What used to happen is that as I got angrier, people backed away from me and gave me room, therefore if my path was clear I would be encouraged to leave. In the end I usually took my anger out on some inanimate object that just happened to be there.

There were also the times when at a party and feeling alone I would have a fake heart attack, which led to concerned people calling an ambulance that would then take me to hospital. My dad was called and by the time he got there the poor overworked doctor had identified that medically there was nothing wrong with me. There never was anything wrong physically, it was just that I was alone and felt unwanted and therefore I needed attention, therefore I manufactured it.

I also used to argue at home to get attention and storm out, with my dad and sometimes my mum or others following. I would run to the nearby motorway bridge and climb up on the barrier, threatening to jump. I had an audience and the attention that I craved. I was never going to jump but they believed I might.

I think the event that sums up this insanity best happened in my early 20s on a Sunday evening. I had been drinking at lunchtime and was already feeling in need of attention and, as the evening progressed and the beer flowed, thing got worse. I remember feeling so alone and unwanted, that I was going to make sure somebody was going to notice me. I made up a story to some of my drinking mates that somebody in another local pub had upset me and I was going to sort them out. This was about attention because I wanted them to feel sorry for me and to come and rescue me. I left the Working Men's Club and headed for the flat of somebody I knew. I convinced or scared him into lending me an empty shotgun. I then drove to the car park of the pub that I'd told my friends the problem was in, hid behind a car and shouted out, 'If you come out I will f…ing shoot you.' I was the only person there who knew that the gun was empty. In time my mates turned up and I let them take the gun and get me away from there before the police turned up. There was no problem. There was just attention seeking. I needed somebody to save me. Never mind the consequences that my actions may have caused, 'just save me'!

Relationships and marriage

Prior to my drinking and during my drinking I had at times been in relationships. They all have a similar narrative to them. I would meet somebody who was nice to me and I liked them. Very quickly I would fall in love with them, buying cards and gifts for them. Every time I thought that this was the person to love and fix me. This was it, I was whole. What I didn't know at that time was that the problem was inside me. I did not believe that anybody could love or want to be with me. I was unlovable. This caused me to slowly sabotage these relationships. I would constantly ask if they loved me and want to know what they were doing without me. I would easily get upset with them at the slightest hint of them not being devoted to me. In truth my expectations were so high, nobody could live up to them. They left, leaving me desolate and pleading for them to return, which of course they didn't, and so I got comfort by pouring my heart out to anybody who I could take hostage to listen. I craved love and attention, while destroying it when it was there.

The other type of relationship I had was with somebody much older than me, who did not mind me turning up full of alcohol. I used to arrive in the early hours of the morning, wondering why I was doing this again. The answer was simple. I needed love and affection. I saw sex as love and therefore for those few moments I was loved. Then came the realisation of the truth of the situation. I would swear to myself that I would never do this again but, just like alcohol, I did. The lady in question fully participated in this relationship and seemed to be quite happy with it. I believe she saw it for what it was. I was a lonely male seeking sex and she was happy in those moments to provide it.

In my late 20s it became clear to me that I needed to get married. Not for love but because of my mum and dad. My behaviour over the years had worn then down. They had had enough of me and talk turned to me moving out. What I needed was a wife and, more importantly, a new carer. Somebody to look after me, to love me, to be there for me, plus I fancied the fringe benefits of marriage.

At the time I was calling the bingo at the local Working Men's Club and my eyes and intention fixed on a lady who regularly went there with her friends for an evening out. After a few drinks one night, I asked her if I could walk her home and to my surprise she said 'Yes'. We were halfway there when we bumped into three children and an Alsatian dog. 'Evening, Mum,' they said, 'who is that bloke with you?' By the end of the evening I found out that she was divorced from her husband who was a very heavy drinker, that she had three children, ranging from 8 to 14 and an Alsatian dog, who did not like men. Any sane single man with no experience of children or the complexities of step-children and ex-husbands would have walked away that first night, but not me. I had decided that I loved her and that I wanted to marry her. If ever a relationship was destined to fail, this was it. I was emotionally just a child and very needy. I would listen to no one, she was the one for me. As far as my drinking goes, this is the point where the walls started closing in on me. I never stopped drinking but moved the bar indoors and took up drinking scotch.

As it turned out, my new partner needed me as much as I needed her. She needed somebody to fix, to sort out. In truth, to control. She behaved in a different way to others if I got upset. When I threatened to leave, she would say, 'Go then'. She did not play my game because she was playing one of her own. We had many small break-ups and upsets but she remained resolute. She would not chase me. Instead she waited for me to come back and over time she gradually took control. I would feel unhappy and unloved, I would start to move away but I only got so far and got scared, so I would always go back to her.

There were many difficulties with her children and ex-husband that I would repel from but I always went back. She was in control of me. I was the naughty child and she was the mother. I was afraid of losing her love, she knew that and used it to manage me. She was living her life script and I was living mine. She was the director and I was an actor in the play.

My reward it seemed was that I was allowed to drink at home, and every night I would anesthetise myself. I was drinking more. The pressure was building. I was finding it harder and harder to cope. It was like living in a tunnel with the light at the other end slowly getting further and further away, while my drinking was getting more desperate.

Miraculously we produced twins. They were and are great, but in the early days I remember feeling that I was there, but not ever really present. It was as if life was going on around me. I remember one evening calling Alcoholics Anonymous and talking to somebody. It was going fine until they asked if I had hit my wife. 'No,' I said. If that's what they do then I am not an alcoholic. I had in the past hit my wife with the living room door. I knew she was there. I was angry, so I pushed it hard into her. However, this was not punching. I decided that I was not a real alcoholic yet.

Several months later I found myself at the doctor's. This was because my wife had threatened to throw me out. I could not lose her. She was all I had. I sat there and told the truth. I was scared. I wanted help. Alcohol had beaten me. I told him about incidents that he was aware of because at the time I had gone to him for emotional support. I said, 'On every occasion when I came to see you about how I could not cope with life and you prescribed me medication or sent me to a counsellor or to the psychiatric unit, I was drunk! When I overdosed, I was drunk! When I rolled the car with my children in it, I was drunk! I am always drunk. Doc, please tell me what is an alcoholic?' He looked at me, sat back in his chair and said, 'You are, you are and have always been an alcoholic, right from your very first drink when it changed you.'

This was the first time that I had been honest about my drinking. The truth had set me free. That day, well over 30 years ago, I went to my first Alcoholics Anonymous meeting and I have never had a drink since.

Alcoholics Anonymous and the start of my recovery journey

Recovery from any physical addiction or mental illness is a journey, which may not go smoothly. It is a bit like peeling an onion. At its core is the truth of you. That free young spirit that life affected from such an early age. Around that core are many layers. There is the emotional damage done, the coping strategies developed to deal with the pain. The strategies and substances used to change how you feel. Each different area has many, many layers that have built up over the years and, until those core behaviours change, will carry on building up. My outside layer was my alcoholism and before I could start to recover mentally, I had to rid myself of my alcoholic dependence.

In the recovery programme of Alcoholics Anonymous Big Book there is a sentence that states, 'There are those too who suffer from grave emotional problems, they too can recover if they had the ability to be honest with themselves.' What this means to me is that there are those alcoholics who were fine until they drank and after that they became addicted to alcohol and it affected every area of their lives, including their connection to their own God, higher power or spiritual beliefs. However, once sober they soon regained their senses and became again respected members of society

Then there is another group of alcoholics who suffer from grave emotional problems. I identify emotional problems as those caused due to a variety of traumas during early childhood. This is now recognised as PTSD. What this means to me is that in addition to what every alcoholic has to do, which is to stop drinking, clear up the carnage of their past, and reconnect with their higher power, for alcoholics of my type stopping drinking is but a first step and in some ways the easier step, because changing our core belief systems is very difficult, mainly because it is what we know, what we live by. What at our core we believe ourselves to be. It is our life script.

As I started out on my journey of recovery I was unaware of the challenges that lay ahead, I just wanted to get well. I attended meetings every day and I got myself a sponsor to help me work the 12-step recovery program of Alcoholics Anonymous. Meetings were and still are important to me. It is where alcoholics share their experience, strength and hope. It was in these meeting that for the first time I was able to talk about the fears I had which filled my head. I talked about everything and anything that bothered me. The words and feelings poured out, sometimes angrily and aggressively, but they came out. To my surprise others shared that they had thought and did the things that I had done, but had not done again since they had got sober. I remember the night that I shared that on two different occasions I had slept with men. I said that I had been lonely and needed love, and how those two events had me still questioning if I was gay, even though I was married with two children. After the meeting a fellow came quietly up to me and said, 'I felt the same and did the same, it's okay just don't drink and you won't do it again'. He was right, I never have.

I was not alone anymore, others were like me. I was completing the 12-step program and for a short while thought that I was well. This was short-lived as those same old feelings surfaced again, continuing to impact on every area of my life. I had to be rid of fear and therefore as part of my recovery program I set out to clear up the wreckage of my past. I contacted and agreed to repay all my creditors. I carried out amends to all those I had hurt. I tried to be a better husband, a better son and a better father. To my wife I had become a doormat. I did not argue. I did as I was asked. I believed I was doing amends but instead I had lost my voice and role. I was being walked all over.

During this same period, I smacked one of my children and hurt her. I was concerned that my anger was returning, when in truth it had never left me. My doctor sent me to a group that met in the local psychiatric unit. It was there that I first heard the concept of how childhood experiences impact on our adult lives. The group was intense and discussed abandonment and its consequences. I was attending about the fifth session and I remember getting very angry and frightened in the session, so I left early and went home. Feeling very strange, I went to bed. On awakening in the morning, the world seemed different. I had no fear, I was like a happy child, with a child's voice and child's outlook. I was a child. A free and happy child who felt safe, secure and loved. I kept saying, 'I'm five!'

My wife rang a friend of mine and they took me to hospital. A doctor asked if I knew who the Prime Minister was and what year it was. As I was aware of both they let me go home, with the advice of letting me work through what was happening, but to get in touch if nothing changed. My friend took me to see an

Inner Child Therapist that evening, where I regressed from five years old, to a baby. She explained that in the morning I would be fine, things would be clearer and would return to normal. However, come the following morning I was still five and still cuddling my teddy bear. I now believe that it was at five years old that as a child I decided to hide inside myself, to protect myself. I believe that by then it was already too painful and that I was already damaged.

I can still clearly remember the day that at the age of five life became too painful for me. My mum and dad disappeared one day. My brother and I got up in the morning and they were gone. A neighbour was there getting our breakfast and despite our protestations not a word was said about where they were. Later in the day, after many more enquiries, the neighbour looked down at us and said, 'Your nan's dead! Your mum's mum is dead and they are burying her today.' That was the point that I could face no more pain and hid. That was the first day that I remember that feeling of abandonment and that was the day that my life changed. My parents did what they thought was best for us and them: if only they had known how different my life might have been if they had been well enough to make different choices.

I spent the next week being five years old, and during that week I relived many of my life's experiences but through the eyes of a happy five-year-old child and not the frightened five-year-old child that I had been. I had been given a glimpse of how it was possible to feel, and I wanted it. After that this was always my journey. I had to find the road to emotional freedom and, as I came to believe later, self-love.

New beginning

At this time I was not working because as a result of my drinking I had damaged my spine that required extensive surgery to fix. I used to walk my girls to school and collect them every day on my crutches, while at night I was at AA meetings sharing my anger and pain. Other AA members were frightened of me and kept their distance. There were only a few who I trusted to be near me and they understood me because they had had the same experiences as me and they too felt abandoned. The girls' teacher did not see that person, what she saw was the truth of who I was when she saw me each and every day arriving and leaving with my children. She asked me if I would go into her class to sit and read with the children because, in her opinion, I was a good role model for children. I believed that I was a failure and mentally unwell. She saw a loving father, whom she trusted to read with children. This was a turning point and over time I became more and more involved in the classroom, while at night in AA meetings I continued to expel my demons in a not very subtle way.

It was suggested a while later that I should become a teacher. Believing that they would reject me out of hand I rang my local adult education college and what follows is what was said. 'I am a recovering alcoholic. I have no formal qualifications but it has been suggested by my children's teacher that I would make a good teacher. Can you help?' I was already putting the phone down, convinced of the outcome, when a voice said, 'Yes, we can help. We have just the course for you.'

For the first few months of my college course, I would go home every evening and ring an AA friend of mine, saying, 'I can't go on, this is too hard for me,' and she would say, 'You can do it, just do one day at a time.' So while each day I was attending and achieving on the course, every night I was trying to say that I could not do it. Here was the dilemma. I was doing it, but believed that I couldn't. Then one evening after I had yet again rung her and said that I could not do it, she said, 'I am fed up with this, if you want to leave just leave.' Confronted with the truth what would I do?

I completed the college course and I achieved a distinction for the course and passed both GCSEs with flying colours. When I read these results on the college notice board my old belief system went into overdrive. This was wrong. I cannot get these marks. I am too stupid. I am a failure. I went to the Marks office and explained this to them. The look on their faces will always stay with me. I do not think anybody before had ever argued that their marks were too high.

The following year I started a four-year degree course at University. When I got the letter offering me a place, I did not believe it was real. Each year at University the work got progressively harder. Each time I submitted work I expected to fail and was surprised to pass. I had the same experiences on my teaching practices. Despite the mounting evidence of success, I still did not believe that I could achieve anything.

Everybody including me knew that I could not cope and would fail, therefore I could never celebrate success. I just worked harder because I continually expected not to be able to achieve the next step. This behaviour followed me right through University and when I was awarded a First Class Honours Degree, I again went to the Marks office and challenged it. Despite myself and my beliefs I was achieving and I was changing. I had become a high achiever, well – on paper at least.

It was during my second year at University that I had my second experience of regression. I had sought help from the university counsellor due to the difficulties that I was having with my eldest stepdaughter. I can now say that my insecurities and need for love had led to bad behaviours and manipulation on my part. This had then led to our relationship breaking down completely. I was not aware of this at the time and just thought that she was being awkward and that she did not like me. This was probably true, given how I treated her.

I told the counsellor that I wanted to kill her, just to get her out of the way. He asked me on an anger scale of one to ten, what somebody would have to do for me to want to kill them. I can remember saying, 'If somebody seriously harmed or abused my children, I would want to kill them.' He then asked me how many times that had happened in my life and I said, 'Never.' If this is the worst and it has never happened, why are you saying you want to kill your stepdaughter, given that all she has done is to get in your way because she lives at home and loves her mum? This was the first time that anybody had explained to me what a proportionate response was. We started to list events that made me angry and put them on a scale of one to ten, the aim being for me to be able to respond with a level of anger that was proportionate to the event that had happened. This is a model that I have used many times since.

We were coming towards the end of the session when I felt this change come over me. It was like another person had taken over. A voice that I hardly recognised said, 'Is it alright if I am a girl?' I can remember the counsellor saying that it was okay to be anything that I wanted to be. A great relief came over me and I started to laugh. I laughed uncontrollably for about twenty minutes. The counsellor said that he had never seen anybody laugh as much. When I eventually calmed down, I was younger, much younger. I felt that I was a young teenager of about fifteen years of age and I felt very free. After making sure that I was okay the counsellor gave me a note and sent me back to my classes. The note read something like, *'This person is going through some emotional changes at the moment and is currently acting like a teenager. If he becomes too disruptive please send him back to me and I will look after him.'*

At the end of the day I went back to see him and spent some time with him just relaxing. As the time slowly passed I began to slowly return to my normal self, with my normal voice. By the morning I was an adult again and fully back in the present. I believe that my struggles as a teenager regarding my sexuality were voiced by my inner fifteen-year-old child and that he was elated to find out that he could be whoever he wanted to be. For the first time ever I had been validated, I could be me. This was a huge step in healing the different parts of me that were broken.

At home things were much the same but as I started my first teaching role in a junior school the clouds were beginning to gather. I had started to believe that I deserved a voice at home. I had started to want to be part of conversations and decision making. I wanted to be a full partner. This was met with stiff resistance from my wife and at every opportunity she would say, 'You have not changed. You are still the same.' I was not the same, my frustrations came as a result of her behaviours and actions. In her mind I was always the problem. I was still a child.

To compensate for my insecurities at work I became an overachiever. I was a good teacher and communicator and I was glad to take on additional responsibilities. Within a couple of years I was the Head of Year and Maths Co-ordinator and then I moved to another school as Assistant Head Teacher and Safeguarding lead. I had been there two or three years when my Head Teacher went part-time and I acted up as Acting Head while he was away. It was then suggested that I take the Head Teachers qualification, which I passed, and then the following day I was appointed Head Teacher of my own school.

The beginning of the end

This whole process had taken about nine years and while I evolved and changed, my wife remained that same person that she had always been. By now, however, her behaviours had deteriorated because she was finding it harder to control me as I started to find myself and wanted an adult relationship.

While I was better educated, earned a much better salary and was respected by my peers, inside I still felt the same. That fear and insecurity had never left me, I had just learnt more strategies to manage it. It did escape once. We were expecting Ofsted and at the time I had quite a lot of responsibility. I had been working long hours and in the late afternoon before they were due to arrive I became ill. On arriving home from work I phoned my doctor to explain the symptoms. She said, 'Put the phone down and dial 999 and tell them you are having a heart attack, then sit down and wait for the ambulance.' I was in hospital about a week. It turned out not to be a heart attack. What had happened was that the anxiety I was suffering had caused the muscles around my heart to contract and squeeze my heart, causing the symptoms of a heart attack. In truth, the problem was the same - I still did not believe in me!

You would think that as a Head Teacher I would celebrate my success and enjoy the journey for a little while. Not me, this was my school and failure within it would reflect badly on me. This need to achieve and constantly prove myself was debilitating, every area of my life was suffering. My marriage after twenty-seven years was deteriorating more and more. My wife's behaviours deteriorated as she struggled harder and harder to justify and control me, while I was now able to voice an opinion, to stand my ground, to want to be an equal partner.

Eventually to try and control me she used the only weapon that she had left. She contacted a friend of mind, accusing me of sexually abusing my granddaughter, saying that she was contacting the police and social services. This was on the same day that I had spoken to her about moving into my mum's house for a while, so that we could try and sort our marriage out. She was acting in a vindictive and calculating way, but when you are losing control, you take more and more drastic steps. That was the day that I left the family home and my marriage and that was the day that I had to tell my daughters that their mother had accused me of abusing one of their children, my granddaughter.

It is almost impossible to put into words the impact that these events had on me. The accusation was bad enough but the way it was done and why it was done destroyed a part of me inside. This was betrayal and abandonment way beyond anything that I had experienced before. My children devastated and my family torn apart, and all because I was trying to be a decent human being. I now understand that my wife suffered from her own demons and her need to control, her behaviours and actions driven like mine by fear and rejection. The less I needed a mother and the more I needed a wife, the worse it got for her, until in the end she pushed the destruction button.

While my personal life had fallen apart, I did what I thought best, I kept to my routines and went to work, although now I was living back with my mum. I told my Chair of Governors what had happened and she took advice. She said, 'Currently this is just a verbal threat from an angry wife. If she does go to the authorities we will suspend you, but at the moment she has reported nothing.' It felt like she was trying to still control me. It was like having a guillotine hanging overhead, just waiting for it to fall. There was no truth in any of her accusations but that did not matter, the damage was done. 'Do what I want you to do or the axe will fall on you...' The problem was that I was no longer a child. I was an adult and I had my own mind. A few days later I went on an overnight training course and the despair and loneliness hit me. I did not want to drink, so I would jump. I climbed over the balcony, just wanting everything to end. I was there for ages waiting to be saved but nobody came. Eventually I climbed back and rang an AA friend of mine, who spoke to me for hours until I fell asleep.

The following months were horrible. I lost contact with my children as they struggled to come to terms with what was happening. The anger and pain of what had happened haunted me every minute of every day, and I was still trying to run a school. In truth, because of my growing fears I was people pleasing. I was so alone and frightened that I would do anything for people to like me, so I agreed to almost anything at work, which just caused more difficulties. Each day was like trudging through treacle. I started seeing a counsellor and tried to just keep going, believing that eventually the pain would pass.

While my recollections are of only my own pain at this time, others remember it differently. A very good AA friend of mine, on reading a draft of this text, contacted me to recount his memories of that time. He recalls that while I was clearly having severe difficulties I was still doing my best to help others. At the time he was going through a very difficult relationship problem that he was having great difficulty navigating. He recalls that during this time, I was his rock and that he believes that if I had not been there to support him, something tragic might have happened. I do not remember this. It is another example of how my mind only ever held on to negative thoughts and behaviours which enforced my negative belief system and rejected any thought or action that might have given me hope.

After a few months I bumped into a long-time friend of mine and we started going out. I was in need of love and affection and she had always liked me. This was the first time that I felt the sunlight shine on my spirit. I had somebody and we had each other. It may have been papering over the cracks in my personal life and giving me a reason to get up, but it did not change my feelings regarding school. People just kept asking for and expecting more and more. I retreated further and further into my office.

Endgame

After a while I moved in with my partner and things stabilised for a while, but then her daughter returned home from University. It is fair to say that at that time I could not share somebody's love. You either loved me totally or not at all. My anxieties at home began to grow. All I could see was that it was happening again. I was going to be rejected. I was unlovable. I was not wanted. I was full of jealousy of the love my partner had for her daughter. That love should be mine.

At school I was now avoiding some staff and parents. I was afraid of going out into the playground in case there were problems and then, to add to the pressure, we did not do as well as expected in an Ofsted inspection. I just broke down and cried. I had failed. It did not matter what others said. I was a failure. I had let the school, parents and children down. It was all true. My life script had turned another page and again I was alone and frightened and isolated.

The walls continued closing in and I seemed unable to do anything to stop it. I had tried. I had worked hard. I have done my very best to change and to be a good person. I had kept doing the right thing even under the greatest of pressure. I could see none of this or accept that any of it was not my fault. Throughout all those years despite the successes, promotions and new relationship, I was alone. I was unloved and in my mind nobody wanted me. I was still living by my old script.

My partner and I had been to see her parents for a few days. It had not been easy and I had found myself isolating and ruminating on my failures more and more. On returning home we walked into the house to find what I thought was a huge mess made by her daughter. I internally exploded. I had left the place tidy. My head screamed that she had done this on purpose. She had never wanted me to be with her mum. It was like an emotional dam broke and all my fears and failures poured out through the breach. In a daze I unpacked the car and said to my partner, ''I am done!' I walked out the door knowing that this time I had nowhere to go. I ended up staying at my mum's that night but in the morning she told me that I could not stay there because my brother and his wife were coming to stay. This was the last straw, even my mother did not want me despite knowing and seeing the emotional state that I was in. She was abandoning me again.

I drove to the river and rang my partner. She was very upset with me and kept saying that I had just walked out the door and left her. I tried to explain that if I had stayed I could have done something stupid to her daughter, to her, the house or to myself, so I decided to leave. At that time she could not hear what I was saying as she was so upset herself. I remember a short silence over the phone and a feeling of certainty that I had never experienced before. I said to her 'I have tried but I am out of steps, it's over! I have nowhere else to go!' I ended the call and decided that I was going to the coast to drive into the sea and put a stop to all the pain. I was going to drive me and my car off the end of a pier. At that moment I was very calm and contented to end it all. This was my sanity.

What happened next, I have worked out by piecing things together. I remember very little of it. Evidently my partner kept ringing me and I just kept crying and telling her goodbye. She contacted the police, who tracked my phone, and the next thing I remember is the sound of a police siren that pulled me back to the present. I was nearly at the coast, although I remember nothing of the drive. I remember looking to my right at the policewomen in the car next to me. The lights were flashing and she was waving for me to slow down. I remember thinking to myself that I would not make the pier but I could still drive into a wall. Then I saw the officer's face, she looked younger than my children. I could not harm them. This was about ending my pain, not causing more pain. I slowed and stopped the car, my head in a whirl of emotion and sadness. The officers came towards me and asked me to get out of the car. As I did, everything spun and I passed out. The next thing I remember was being sat in the back of a police car. They drove me to the local hospital. I was exhausted and spent. Just end this. Turn the light off and let me sleep. I wanted the end and would find a way to achieve it.

I was very quickly seen by a doctor and admitted into hospital. I was sedated and remember lying on a bed, surrounded by curtains, with police officers in attendance due to me being a serious suicide risk and then my partner arrived, only this time I did not want rescuing, I just wanted to die. Another doctor appeared and injected me in the arm and slowly peace arrived as I drifted off into what I hoped would be oblivion, but in truth was simply to sleep. Little did I know that on awakening my life as I knew it would forever change.

Getting off the wheel of life

Over the next thirty-six hours I was slowly moved back to my local psychiatric unit nearer to my home. There was a one-day stopover in a unit where I was medicated to help me settle down. I was monitored constantly. Finally I arrived at the psychiatric unit at the local hospital and was admitted onto a locked ward. I remember very little about those first few days except that I kept being hit by waves and waves of uncontrollable emotion and fear. The psychiatrist there assessed me and placed me on 50mg of Sertraline. He also informed me that I had PTSD. This made me feel like a fraud because I always believed that PTSD was what soldiers suffered from as a result of their involvement in a war.

I remember finding a quiet room and just sitting there. I found a couple of books and started to read. I craved peace and quiet and this room became my haven, a place of safety and solitude. The difficulty was that every time I was asked about what had happened to me or had a random thought from the past drift through my mind, the waves of emotion hit me again and again until eventually I was put on a dose of 200mg of Sertraline a day, and that seemed to keep the waves at a manageable level, so that I could sleep and have some peace in my mind.

While there a few things happened that were to prove

pivotal in how I was to slowly rebuild my life. My mother and sister live within five miles of the hospital and while my brother lives further away, he was always visiting the area. At no point during my time in hospital did any of them come to visit me. Despite all that I had done over time to support them and despite their pronouncements of love. None of them came. Love is not a word but an action and by theirs they had made their true feelings clear.

My partner came to see me every few days. She had been traumatised by what had happened to me and was also dealing with her daughter, who was very angry with me, but she came. Every time she came she brought me Diet Coke and chocolate that I used to take to my little room and consume while reading my books. I read or slept from morning to night and the only time that I was disturbed was to tell me it was mealtime.

The other very important thing that happened was for the first time since my marriage break-up my twin daughters came to see me. They said that they loved me and how they wanted to help. I had never told them the difficulties that I was having regarding the end of my marriage and they said that they had believed that I was strong enough to deal with the past and move on. We were both wrong. I should have made more effort to talk to them and they could have checked how I was. However, they were there now and from believing that they did not care, the truth emerged and we were able to move on. My Alcoholics Anonymous friends came to see me and helped me get through each day, and all of them demonstrated the action of love, which to this day I have never forgotten.

It was during my second week there that I had my first revelation of what I needed to do, even if at that point I did not know how to do it. I went to an art therapy group where we were encouraged to use the materials available to produce a piece of art and then we would all talk about it. Using chalks I drew two islands surrounded by water, one was small, black and foreboding, while the larger was full of colour. Between them was a narrow bridge. The patients all discussed each piece of artwork and then the artist was asked to describe what it meant to them. Eventually it came to my piece of work and everybody discussed what they thought, and then I was asked to explain it. I said that the dark island was where I existed and that it was full of fear and self-loathing. I went on to talk about the larger brighter island being made of love, and that the bridge was a path that I wanted to cross so that I could enjoy life. The therapist asked me what I would do with the bridge once I had crossed it. I never replied and she began to move on to another piece of work. Over the next few minutes, a great anxiety and frustration built up in me until I jumped off my stool, walked to the front and ripped the corner of my picture, tearing down the bridge and the dark island. 'What are you doing?' she asked. I remember that I was crying and shaking and said, 'I am going to cross the bridge and then blow it and the bloody dark island up so that I can never go back there.' This was the first time that I had ever thought of the concept of not living in fear but of choosing to live in love. This image became a cornerstone of what my future journey was going to be.

I explained this piece of art to my clinical psychologist and she asked if after I left hospital I would like to return each week to see her, so that we could explore this journey. The future work that I did with the psychologist is another cornerstone in my recovery. The other thing that happened is that as I was unable to return to my partner's home, due to the trauma that I had caused and the impact that had had on my partner and her daughter, my daughter then asked if I wanted to stay with her.

Due to my breakdown a healing between my twin girls and me had taken place and I was offered sanctuary by my daughter. This is the third cornerstone of my recovery because my daughter gave me a safe environment where I was able to very slowly over several months recuperate. My recuperation took the form of walking the dog, who became my best friend, and sitting in the garden or my room reading books. It was the most precious of times because it enabled my mind to slow and settle down and for the first time to see the truth of who I really was.

It was towards the end of my stay in hospital that my friend came to take me out for coffee. I had received permission to leave the unit and to walk across the road to a coffee shop. What I did not know is what was said to my friend when he came to pick me up. One of the nurses said to him in no uncertain terms, 'If he needs cutlery make sure you get it for him and afterwards make sure you put it over the counter at the end. Under no circumstances can you let him slip a knife into his pocket.' Evidently I also insisted on sitting in the corner with my back to the wall so that I could make sure that nobody crept up on me. He was quite taken aback by the concerns of the staff and my behaviour, and looking back this simple outing for coffee demonstrates how I was and how at risk others thought I was. It is a sobering memory and one I never want to repeat.

Life script

During this recuperation time I saw the clinical psychologist every week. For the first few sessions I regurgitated to her the trials and tribulations of my life. How I believed I was a failure. How I believed that nobody liked me. How I believed that I was unloved. How fearful I was. How I had no self-worth. I laid myself bare in front of her, believing that this was who I was and that nothing could change that.

Then at the start on one session she said to me, 'Is what you are telling me really the truth of you?' 'This is how I feel,' I replied. 'Yes,' she said, 'I understand that, but is this the truth of you?' I looked at her, confused; of course this was me. This is how I felt and everybody knew what I was like.

She then said, 'Then how do you explain the fact that you played sport and football from a young age and were very successful? How do you explain your athletic achievements? Is not 98% in a cycling proficiency test a success? Did you not look after your sister while your mother was ill? Did you not recover from a spinal injury and walk again? Did not your children's teachers see you as a good role model and ask you to help other children? Did you not get accepted into college, get a distinction and two qualifications at the end of the course? Where you not accepted into University, graduating four years later with a First Class Honours degree? Did you not become a teacher, then a Deputy Head Teacher, then a Headmaster? Did you not for a time run two schools and serve on the schools' governing bodies? Did you not survive your wife's accusations about you and the breakdown of relationships with your daughters? Are you even now not striving to overcome your difficulties? How can this be failure?'

I had no answer. These were things that I had done but never celebrated. Whatever I did, the same overriding feelings had persisted. I was not good enough! I could have done better! I was not loved!

Here was the dichotomy. The evidence laid out in front of me said that I had achieved and was a success, but my inner voice, my belief system, screamed at me that I was not. My psychologist explained to me that early on in life I had developed beliefs about myself and acted in that way, so others had come to believe it and to treat me that way. Whatever I had achieved had been followed by uttering the word 'but'. I got 98% in my cycling test but my brother and sister got more. I got a distinction at college but I did not really deserve it. I got a job as a Deputy Head Teacher but only because I knew somebody there and nobody else applied. Throughout my life I had never celebrated or owned my achievements. I had belittled myself. I had always set my expectations far too high and never accepted that what I had achieved was good enough. All my relationships where based on how much people should have loved me and what they should do to prove their love to me. The expectations that I placed on them always meant that they failed and I was abandoned again. Could this be true? Was I really the architect and creator of my own destruction? Over many years I had come to believe and created what I thought I was. Could all this be a lie?

Then came a moment of awakening, as I was asked, 'Who do you want to be?' This was the fourth cornerstone. I decide that I wanted to live in love not fear. I could feel safe and there could be peace and quiet in the environment that I lived in. I had been invited to and chosen who I now wanted to be.

Over the next few weeks we discussed many areas of belief and behaviours in my life. We talked about my mother, brother and sister and how over many years I had done so much to help them, to make them love me. We looked at what they had given me in return and how my actions had led to them expecting me to do anything they asked. These were one-way relationships and this had been clearly demonstrated when none of them came to see me in hospital.

Over the last few months I have started visiting my mum again. Mainly because she is nearly ninety and I would not want her to die without being able to see her oldest son. We laugh and joke now and have a good time. I take each visit as it comes and focus on the time and effort my mum gave freely to me as I was growing up. I also navigate myself away from any conversations that might bring up the past.

We looked at my management style in school and my relationships with the parents. I talked about collaborative leadership but in truth I agreed to most things that people wanted, especially if the request came from powerful outspoken women. I had realised by then that I was afraid to upset them and wanted them to like me. I needed women to like me, this was to fill the hole left in me by my perception of my mother's lack of love for me. This behaviour just created the same problems over and over again. They just asked for and expected more and more. I could not stand up to them or deliver what they wanted. I was not leading but being led. I enabled then to take nearly everything that they wanted and they gave nothing in return. I felt let down and abandoned, but I had created it. I had the same problem with parents, mothers especially. They frightened me as I did not want to upset them, so I made concession after concession to them until eventually I was hiding in my office to avoid them, as well as most of the staff.

We discussed how whatever I achieved in life was never going to be good enough, and how the expectations I set for myself were almost guaranteed to fail. My belief system had a default setting of failure, so whatever I did was never going to be good enough and therefore I was not good enough.

We looked at my marriage and why I got married. I had no idea about adult relationships. What I wanted was not a wife but a new mum with fringe benefits. It was probably doomed to fail from the start. I could not share love. You had to love me. This led to constant issues with my bad behaviour in trying to get her attention and my attempts to drive a wedge between her and her children. If you don't love me and only me, you don't love me! We identified how over many recent years I had done what I was told to do. I was a doormat.

The problems had developed as my professional life progressed. It was a marriage based on my childish needs and her need to control. Once I started to change due to Alcoholics Anonymous and my career it was doomed. The whole marriage was based on my need for love and a lie. What hope did it ever really have?

We looked at my relationship with my current partner and despite all my efforts, how when her daughter came home I could not cope with it. With the thought that she may love her daughter more than me. How in all my relationships over time I had been dependent on the love of others to make me feel safe and okay. How eventually my beliefs, behaviours and jealousy had destroyed them. It seemed clear that I needed to be able to love myself. I needed to learn to be able to live alone. Only when I had achieved these things could I begin to develop a healthy adult relationship with a loving partner.

So here were the first things that I needed to do, to find out who I wanted to be. The first thing that I did was to write to my mother, brother and sister, saying to them that I was breaking all contact with them because love is not a word, but an action. By their actions while I was in hospital they did not demonstrate love for me and that going forward I did not want people in my life who did not love me.

After six months my employers contacted me regarding the termination of my contract. For the first time I explained to the Chair of Governors how the job made me feel and that I was not in my opinion suitable for the role any more. It is interesting that despite my efforts to make the staff and parents respect and like me, nobody except the Chair of Governors has ever contacted me to see how I am. Again the pattern is the same, I give all that I can to get people to like me and in the end I am left alone. In the end we agreed a compromise agreement and I left the role. I cannot explain the weight that lifted off of me and how free it made me feel. The thought of having to walk back through those school doors used to bring me out in a cold sweat. Funnily enough I did recognise at this point how my constant drive to achieve more had helped me accumulate a good teacher's pension that now is at the core of my financial stability.

It was also clear that to find myself, I needed to live on my own. This is because I had always relied on others for my safety and comfort and to be the person that I wanted to be I had to live on my own to learn to love myself. My partner agreed with this and after looking for a while, I found myself a lovely little granny annex to live in, where I am now very happy. I have learnt to look after myself, sit with my feelings and to be content on my own. I live alone but I now never feel lonely.

My wife was a much more difficult problem to deal with. The first thing that I did was to contact an online divorce company, who managed the divorce for me. I was very frightened throughout this process as I was sure that she would contact me and tell me off, but it needed to be done, especially if I was going to become my own man. Over time I have come to terms with her actions and now accept that she had her problems as much as I had mine. I recently wrote to her and said that I forgave her. I did this to help me let it go. It is now just a sad memory from the past.

Once settled into my new home, I decided that I wanted to do what I liked doing best, which was helping people. Not for me but to help them. Given my mental health experiences I applied for and got a job as a peer support worker working for a mental health charity. To give me the time to do things that I want to do, to help me look after myself, I work part time for three days a week. This is enough for my head to cope with and the money I earn helps me live my life in the way that I want to live it.

The last thing that I decided to do was to look after me, which is something that I have never done. I make time to talk to my close AA friends who have stuck with me throughout this journey. I wanted to get fit and lose some weight so I bought a bicycle and cycle at least once every week. I have this seventeen-mile circuit that goes along the river and through a royal park. I love people watching and the deer in the park are a constant joy. I do not time it. It is not a race. I am not trying to improve each day. I am simply out enjoying a ride, whatever the weather.

To keep my body in shape I visit a physiotherapist every week and over time my body and especially my spine has improved, until now I look forward every week to forty minutes of quiet meditation while I receive a treatment of acupuncture. If you have not tried it you should, it is great in lots of different ways. I also make time to read my books and watch some telly. I also like visiting the National Trust and the seaside and once a week I attend an AA meeting, just to remember where I used to be. It fills me with such gratitude.

My partner and I are still together and both enjoy our lives. We now each live our own lives and spend good quality time together. I believe that finally I have found true love and we love each other just the way we are. Our plan eventually is to retire to the West Country together and at that point we will live together, but until then I am quite content the way things are.

I moved into my new home about three years ago and by the end of the first year I was for the very first time in my life making choices based on what I wanted and thought was best for me. I am not a selfish person by nature, but now I always put me and my needs first. I found as time passed that I was living a slower life. I am not always racing to finish something or looking for the next thing to do. I found that over time I had started to not try and please everybody, but place my needs first. I was experiencing glimpses of something that I had never had before, and that was balance! With balance came time. Time to rest and time to enjoy the moment. Do not be deceived – the changes outlined above were difficult and at times very challenging. Many times I felt that I was slipping back into my old ways but I stuck at it and sat with the pain. I had made a start but there was still more to be done.

My life script

The changes that I have outlined so far are physical and practical challenges, which gave me space, quiet and balance. However, they had not in any way challenged the core issue of my own destructive personal belief system. During all my previous years of trying to solve my mental health problems nobody had ever presented me with a solution. What I had experienced was a variety of coping strategies, sticking plasters, you might say. All that happened over time is that the plaster faded away and the wounds were still there, and as a result I had used alcohol, self-harm, food, relationships and self-seeking behaviours, just to manage and dull the pain. Now in my work as a peer mentor, I saw the same pattern. Clients again and again telling me that nothing really helped them. Things like wellbeing, meditation, affirmations were temporary. What they wanted was a solution to their thinking and beliefs about themselves.

I started to use an AA expression which was 'Just for today'. Just for today you can walk away from a problem. Just for today you can have a routine in your life. This developed into 'Let's make a plan for today'. A plan that describes how you want to behave and feel in that day. What I discovered was that if my clients were given an alternative way to live, think and behave, in the short term there was change. When each week we identified and celebrated that change, however small, it gave clients the belief and confidence to try it for another day. This was a new concept to me. In small ways we were rewriting their life scripts that they had lived by for years. Change was possible. Not just masking the wound but actual healing.

It was at this time that I began to look at Inner Child Healing. This was something that I had heard of before and was aware of but that I had no clear understanding of. I bought the book *Homecoming* by John Bradshaw, who like me has suffered a lifetime of emotional pain and alcoholism. What I learnt empowered me. Here was the reason for my pain and a solution. I researched deeper into the subject and completed an on-line course at the Centre of Excellence. It was called the *Inner Child Healing Diploma*. I also read other material by Catherine Taylor M.A &M.F.C.C (*The Inner Child*) and Lucia Capacchione PH.D. (*Recovery of Your Inner Child*)

What they described is the powerful impact that parents have on their offspring and most importantly how their behaviours and interactions imprint themselves onto the young mind. As an educator I was aware that studies had suggested that 80% of learning in children happens at home. I also knew that apart from things like early sounds and the ability to swallow, children's minds are like a blank sheet of paper. They are sponges waiting to learn. It is what parents and carers teach them and what they come to believe is true that forms the basis of who they will be and how they will feel. It is parents and carers who imprint onto those young vulnerable minds their first and only life script. It is that script that drives their personal beliefs and emotional responses. It is that life script that defines who they are and how they view ourselves. Then by those actions and responses when interacting with others they enforce those beliefs in themselves and those around us. The fact is that once embedded as a child that life script will drive them for a lifetime.

If, when the child is born and the mother is emotionally well, a bonding takes place that never breaks, the child feels secure and safe. Then if the child's experiences continue to be nurturing and loving from those who surround the child, the child will feel loved and therefore love itself. This is the journey for the majority of children; they are safe and sound in the knowledge that they are loved and as a result they love themselves. This is what helps children to overcome the trips and falls of early life and their first interactions at school. They may get hurt, not everybody may like them, they may make mistakes; however, they have resilience because they live in and are surrounded by love. They can lose at games, get upset with adults but all will be okay, because at their core they feel love. This sound and secure upbringing is their life script. They develop the ability to overcome difficulties and setbacks, they have a level of self-belief and self-esteem. They feel confident. They are plugged into love and once established they become rounded children, who are more likely to achieve.

But what of the rest? While everybody's early experiences are different the result and impact are basically the same. What I have previously shared with you is the result of what happened to me due to my experiences. However, there are countless other examples and experiences that have damaged so many young lives. I also need to say at this point that while I used to blame my parents, I no longer do. They only had the experiences and tools that they had learnt about parenting and that was given to them by their parents. Abandonment is a family illness and unless the cycle is broken it will continue from generation to generation.

In their own way my parents loved me. However, they could not demonstrate or give the sort of love that a young impressionable child needed. It is not difficult to understand why given their upbringings they found emotional love and bonding difficult. Mum was the child of alcoholics and had an abusive and deprived upbringing and my father's parents had survived two world wars and lost several babies including twins during childbirth. It is no wonder that his view of love was very practical – how could it not be, with all the trauma and pain he and his parents had suffered? Into this was born a chubby, healthy baby boy with a fine pair of lungs and the need to feel loved and to be made to feel secure. Unfortunately that was not my experience. My mum was never able to bond with me and never has, and my dad kept his distance, to my knowledge never cuddling me. How would any young child react to this? I was being denied the feelings of security and emotional love that every child requires. I was alone and frightened. I did not feel secure. I felt unloved and had no way of loving myself.

I began to develop behaviours to get attention, even if that meant that I did something wrong. While I have very few memories of this time, I can say that my earliest emotions and recollections are those of fear and loneliness. I have discussed earlier my childhood experiences and how they impacted on me. There are, however, two key events that enforced and heightened my sense of loss and abandonment.

The first event was the birth of my brother, when I was eighteen months old. I have heard this called the *'off the knee child'*. This is because as a toddler I was moved aside onto the floor, playpen or pram, so that this new baby could sit on mother's knee. Quite normal, I hear you say, and yes, it is. However, to the abandoned child it is a further dagger to the heart. I received less attention, felt more isolated and as a result my attention-seeking behaviours increased, leading to more crying and more time alone in my pram or bed.

My brother observed and learnt from me how not to behave if you want to be able to sit on mother's knee. He faced the same difficulties as me regarding our parents, but in his case he learnt how to win parental affection and what to do to keep me on the outside. My brother has always in my view behaved as if he is better than me and has acted that way towards me for all of his life. As children we used to play football outside our house and if he was losing, he would say something to upset me. He would then run indoors with me chasing him. 'It's not fair,' he used to shout at mum. 'He is bigger than me and he is going to hurt me.' The result? I got told off and he got the attention. I fell for this behaviour for years and until recently never knew why he looked down on me and why I was so angry with him. It's simple – we were playing the same roles that had developed early in life. We were living our own life scripts.

The other event happened when I was twelve years old and my sister was born. Now I was competing with two siblings and the baby was a girl and the apple of my father's eye. My mother developed post-natal depression, which further strained our relationship, and on top of that because of my need to make people love me, I became her carer. I remember getting upset as all her friends came round to see the baby and play with it, while I was left on the outside, unwanted and unloved. Well, that is how I remember feeling. On another occasion I remember changing her nappy and lifting her up to look at how well I had done. She smiled and emptied her bowel into the nappy, which was not tight enough, and runny yellow poo ran out the sides of her nappy and down her leg. 'Look what you have done!' my mother cried. I tried. I failed. Life was not fair and yet again by trying to please somebody I have caused myself a problem. Again it's interesting that my sister seems to have learnt from observing me and my brother because she has the same outlook and attitude as my brother. In truth it is nobody's fault, we are all just actors playing the part written for us in our life script.

The script was written and learnt long before these events took place. I was living the life of an abandoned and unwanted child, who I believed was unloved, did not love himself and saw failure at every turn. Whatever I have done in the past or achieved, has been viewed through the eyes and emotions of that damaged child.

I have also not been served well by the way that I remember things, which seems to be repeated in many other damaged adults that I know. My brain is like a sieve, achievement and positive thoughts just fall right through it, while magically it catches all my negative thoughts and files them away to be used at a later date. An example of this is something that happened when I was seven years old. My mother bought us a raffle ticket each at the school fête and said that if one of us happened to win, we would both have to share the money. My ticket won and my brother went to great lengths to say that he was getting half my money, and if he didn't it would not be fair. I saw this as unfair and got very upset. I had won, the money was mine. My dad decreed that my share of the winnings would be put towards our new house that we were moving into. I think the amount was five shillings or sixty old pennies. To anybody today it was 25 pence.

Many years later when I was ranting about not being loved and about to storm out of the house at about fifteen years old, I said, 'And another thing, you can give me my share of the money that you stole for the house or I will take a part of the house with me. It's not fair.' Attack and punish was something that I repeated over and over again. The aim was to make others feel guilty so that they would love me more. I never learnt that this does not work, it just further enforces existing beliefs. I was to repeat the stolen money statement many times more, using this and other past experiences to justify a behaviour or belief and to punish others, mostly my mother.

I have now come to understand that it is impossible to change my first unconscious thought, which is always based on fear and low self-esteem as my frightened inner child cries out in emotional pain. However, with practice I have learn to not act on it. I learnt to develop a different second thought that is based on love not fear, and this second thought is the doorway to freedom.

Quietening my inner child

If you watch a toddler who is upset, they have little control over themselves. They cry, scream and throw themselves about, telling their carers that they hate them. I was still behaving like this into my thirties. I may have had the size and strength of a fully grown man but my emotional responses were being driven by that little frightened child inside. I had never emotionally grown up. I was still in the place of loneliness and fear. While the behaviours may sound extreme, just watch any adult who is emotionally out of control and what you are really seeing are the responses of the toddler inside them. If I was going to change or attempt to change my belief system, which is at the very core of me, I had to initially find a way to calm that frightened child.

The early decisions that I made about my family, my job and where I lived had helped because it had removed some of my biggest fears. If you like, I had peeled away one layer of anxiety that I had built up inside me to help protect my inner child. Those very barriers were what my inner child's fears and anxieties fed off, which perpetuated my cycle of destructive behaviours, by reliving my life script over and over again. It was clear, I had to make my child feel safe and loved. To help little me to understand what I was doing I created pieces of art, that depicted love not fear, and wrote loving statements to him on them. I love you little me, I will protect and take care of you. I then created a safe space in my home. It has a reclining chair, cushions, a blanket and a teddy bear. I used to sit there every day talking to my younger self, gently soothing his fears and encouraging him to look beyond the darkness and into the light. Telling him that I loved him and would protect him. We had quiet bonding time together. I was healing myself by parenting my own inner child.

In my mind I created an imaginary place that we used to visit. We started off sitting at the back of a cave, while in the distance we could see a sandy beach. Over time as we felt safer we edged our way to the cave opening and then out into the light, but still never straying far from the entrance. I always knew how safe my inner child felt because on a bad day we were back in the cave and had to start the journey into the light over again. We did this together, always together with the adult me nurturing and reassuring little me. If I return there now as I occasionally do, we are playing in the sand or swimming in the sea and I haven't seen the cave entrance for ages. I believe that means that little me feels safe and secure in the knowledge that I will always love and protect him. He feels safe to play in the sunlight.

Another thing that I have done is write letters to little me. The first one I wrote was written using my dominant hand, in my case my left hand. I explained to him that I knew how he felt and that I was sad that I had been unable to look after and love him properly but that now I was going to protect and love him. I would then sit in my safe place and read the letter to him. After some quiet time I gave him the opportunity to reply. I simply placed the pen in my non-dominant hand, my right hand, and wrote whatever my inner child wanted me to say. In this way I learnt how he felt about things and I was able to find ways to calm him. One example was that driving too fast scared him and so I slowed down a bit and he felt safer. I was able to build a trust with him as more layers fell away and he saw and felt safe in the sunlight. I still take time to settle my inner self and to talk to him. After all, I am the parent and my role is to always protect and keep him safe.

Over time I have been able to quieten my inner voice, and if he ever feels distressed now I am able to sit quietly for a few minutes and settle him. Sometimes this is as simple as slowing my breathing down while mentally cuddling him. In the book *Homecoming* and in other such texts there are various other strategies to help you calm and heal your inner child.

I could now, with love, calm my inner child, which meant that I was not as hypersensitive as I had been when the little fellow was in charge. However, I still had that negative first thought that my life script had given me. If I was a computer the solution would be easy. I could simply wipe the memory and reload a new programme. This is of course not possible with the mind as it retains old memories. So if I could not wipe away the old script, what I could do was to write myself a new script based on the truth of who I am today.

The new life script

This realisation for the first time in my life gave me a choice. I could hold on to the negative first thought, then just let the child take over and go down that same old negative pathway, repeating old behaviours and beliefs. Nothing changes if nothing changes. The alternative was to write myself a new life script, starting from the truth of who I am today in the knowledge that I could manage my inner child in a loving and nurturing way. I could decide how I wanted to feel and how I wanted to act. I could begin again, a new life, with a new life script.

The journey would not be easy, I might sometimes revert to old behaviours, but this was okay, it is the way we learn. New understanding and beliefs are not achieved by getting things right but by getting it wrong. I could learn in a loving way to reflect on any situation, looking at what had happened and why. Then brushing myself off I could simply try again, in the knowledge that I had at least learnt how not to do something. Slowly, sometimes very slowly, the new script would change me and with that I would evolve. Slowly love would be able to take over and I could begin to feel and view the world and its people in a different way. I would learn to love myself and therefore I could love and accept others because I was now a loving creature, living in the sunlight of life.

Now for the first time I had a choice. Now I had the power to begin again. To write a new life script based on the truth of who I really am and what I have achieved. A script based on love and not pain. A script that is of my own making and not one created by others. I must never ever forget, there is no fear in front of me that is more powerful than the love of self and a new found self-belief that is inside of me and part of who I truly am now.

This is what I did. I set some time aside in a quiet, calm place. I sat down and got comfortable and I spent time making sure that my inner child was settled. I explained to him that we were both about to embark on a new journey of freedom and love, based not on the fears and anxieties of the past but on the truth of who we are today.

When I was ready I took a sheet of new clean paper, writing the heading: *What have I achieved for myself in my life so far?* And then down the left hand side of the sheet I simply listed every one of my achievements that I could remember.

I wrote things like:

What have I achieved for myself in my life?	
I learnt to walk	
I leant to talk	
I learnt to read, write, and spell	
I learnt to do maths	
I learnt to swim	
I passed my cycling test	
I got two GCSEs	
I learnt to drive	
I am a father	
I pay my bills	
I have a good job	
I do not owe money to anybody.	
I continue listing every achievement no matter how small it had seemed at the time.	

When I had completed my list I wrote in the heading of the second column: *How did this achievement make me feel?* And then down the right hand side of the column I wrote how each achievement that I listed made me feel.

It looked something like this:

What have I achieved for myself in my life?	How did this achievement make me feel?
I learnt to walk	I kept falling down but in the end I did it.
I leant to talk	I remember the first time that I said 'dad'. It was great, he smiled.
I learnt to read, write, and spell	I used to love reading with my mum at bedtime. I was so proud when I could write and spell my own name.
I learnt to swim I passed my cycling test I learnt to drive	It was great when I swam from the side of the pool to my dad. I remember how mum smiled at me. It was great to have the freedom to go where and when I liked.
I am a father	I was so proud when I saw my daughters I cried with happiness.
I continued listing every achievement no matter how small.	*I continued to list how every achievement made me feel.*

When the sheet was completed I saw the truth of my life. A life viewed from the position of love and not fear. This was the truth of me, set free from the beliefs of my old life script. I was a success. I had achieved. My life did have meaning.

Next I looked at the truth of me today. I wrote two new headings; *What have I achieved today or this week? How do my achievements make me feel?*

For example:

What have I achieved today or this week?	How do my achievements make me feel?
I bathed my children last night	It was great to spend quality time with the kids. I am so lucky to be a parent.
I visited my mum and dad	I do whatever I can do to help them, just look at the things they did for me.
I have arrived on time for work every day this week	I am trustworthy and loyal.
I dealt with a problem with the car	I was so pleased that I kept calm and didn't get angry.
I continued listing every achievement no matter how small.	*I continued to list how every achievement made me feel.*

This was the truth of me, no matter what the inner voices of gloom had said. In black and white, I had listed my achievements and most importantly how I really felt about them. The truth had set me free.

This is who I am today. This is the truth of me and the new foundations on which I could create my own new life script, which will be based in love, because now I live in love and love of myself.

Writing your new life script

Most of us have big issues that fill our minds. One of mine was my mother. The messages that I had lived with kept repeating in my head: I am not good enough; she does not love me; I must have done something really bad in the past; it's my fault, nobody loves me. These messages were at the core of my old life script. If I was going to live in love, I had to have a new plan, a new script to deal with this in a loving and not fearful way. This is what I did.

I created a new grid for every major problem in my life, my mother, my job, my inability to live alone, my brother and sister. These were the large boulders in my mind that blocked the sunlight of love getting in. For each problem area, I created a grid and I tried to make sure that I only used positive language within it. I wrote the three headings below, based on how my true loving self, wanted to feel about her today.

As I remember it looked something like this:

What is the problem? My mother		
How do I want to feel about my mum?	What action can I take to help me feel the way that I want to feel about her?	What language can I use to myself and my mum to help me feel the way that I want to feel about her?
I want to have a voice and put boundaries in place when she puts me down.	When she says that I am fat, I am going to hold the palm of my hand up towards her and stop her talking, and say, 'That is not true, Mum, in fact I am working hard to make sure that does not happen.'	To myself: I am not putting weight on. I exercise and watch my diet. This is not true. To my mum: Mum, this is simply not true. I am happy with my weight and how I maintain it.
I want to be happy to see her.	I can remember all the things she did for me and how she looked after me. I can remember that she is doing the best she can, given that she only had her own life script to live by. I can limit the frequency and length of my visits. If I show and demonstrate love it will help. I will cuddle her and give her a kiss when I leave	Alan, be grateful that you have a mum who looked after you. Remember all the little jobs she worked so that we had nice things. Mum is doing the best she can. Remember what her childhood was like; I was never treated that badly.

I continued to complete the columns until I had a plan for how I wanted to feel about and act around my mum. Like any script, I took time to learn it and when ready I put it into practice. As a result I now enjoy my managed visits to see my mum. She has not changed, but I have. I think over time the script will change. To remember it I just have to read and rehearse it before I visit her and then, whenever my first thought of negativity appears in my mind, I simply say to myself, 'Love not Fear'. By doing this I remember to use my new script. Sometimes I forget but I find that in a short while I remember because the pain and negativity start to return. This is like a slap in the face that reminds me of the need to use my new script again.

I created a plan or life script for every major problem in my life and I found that the more I practised it the better things got, and the more I felt the way that I wanted to. I was starting to see the world through loving eyes and as I did, life improved.

Once I had completed my new scripts for the major difficulties in my life, I set about creating a life script for how I wanted to feel in my life on a day-to-day basis. I laid out my grid with these headings; *How do I want to feel in my life? What actions could I take to help me feel this way? What language could I use about myself and to others to help me feel this way?*

It looked something like this:

How do I want to feel every day? List all the feelings that I want to embrace.	What actions can I take to help me feel this way?	What language should I use about myself and to others to help me feel this way?
Safe	Make a plan before I do something that worries me. Take my time and don't get raced. Look after little me. If I get worried ask for help.	I can do this, just stick with the plan. This will be okay. It's never as bad as I think it is. It's okay little me, I have got you. Please can you help me.
Balanced	Do not do too much. I will create a plan for the day that gives me down time. I will say no to things that I did not want to do. I will always give myself time and prepare properly. I will make sure that I have a daily routine. I will not go to sleep with a problem on my mind. I will write it down to deal with tomorrow.	This is the first time that I have done this, can you help me please?? I have a plan and I am following it. It is good for me to eat regularly. Remember to move at your own pace, it helps you to maintain balance. I am unable to do this for you today as I am already committed to something else. It is alright to say no. Is it my emotional balance that is important?
Happy		
Loved		
Confident		
I listed every positive feeling that I wanted to experience in my day	*I completed this column for every feeling*	*I completed this column for every feeling*

When I had completed the grids I had a plan for my new life script. This model has helped me move towards being the person that I want to be. I have identified the truth of me. I had created a new life script that reflected the person that I wanted to be. All that I have to do now each day is to practise it and learn to live my script.

Over time the negative self has quietened down but I am ever vigilant for that negative first thought so that I can say 'love' not 'fear'. This simple statement helps me remember that I now live by a new loving life script. A day at a time this is enabling me to become the person that I have always wanted to be. A happy contented member of society, who is contented with his lot. I have achieved what I never thought was possible. I have rewritten my life script. I have learnt to love me and life itself. I am healed. To keep this, all that I have to do is to practise every day. I doubt that I will ever be perfect, but that's not the point. Its practice not perfection that enables me to greet nearly every new day with a smile. In time, when this script is fully embedded and if I want to achieve more, all that I have to do is to write another new life script, which can only further enrich my life.

Other actions that I have taken

Over many years I have taken several different steps that helped me eventually to find true inner peace and contentment. If like me you find that you need additional support I would encourage you to find it. Below I have listed the support that I sought and am so grateful for.

I saw several counsellors during my adult life to help me understand and to take some of the power out of the trauma that I have suffered.

I have sought at different times the help of several NHS mental health services which at different times have saved my life.

I have sought medical advice and medication over many years to help me manage and reduce my high levels of stress and anxiety.

I have used the emergency support numbers for organisations such as the Samaritans who, late at night when the dark thoughts are closing in, have been there to offer a kind ear, help and support.

Finally I sought help for Alcoholics Anonymous to help me rid myself of the addiction of alcohol, which enabled me to think clearly and face life on life's terms. It has been the support of other members of AA and the AA programme itself that has proved to be the bedrock of my recovery.

A note to the reader

If after reading this you feel that, like me, you are a prisoner of your own life script and that your life has been hindered by it, then I would suggest that you make a decision today to embark on your own journey to find out who you really are. If you are lucky like me, you will find many fellow travellers seeking the same freedoms. They may travel with you for a while but please never forget that this is your journey of discovery and in the end you have to walk it for yourself. I wish you well as you leave the darkness with your eyes firmly fixed on the sunlight that is just over the horizon.

In the end I was never really alone

Looking back over time it is very clear to me now that many, many people helped me at different times and for different periods of time. They have supported and cajoled me as I have travelled this journey. There are far too many to mention them all and it would be ungenerous to name just a few, so to each and every one of you: I Thank You. Each of you in different ways are part of my journey and in the end part of my success. I dedicate the rest of my life to supporting others as you supported me, so that they too may find freedom from self.

Bibliography:

Homecoming. John Bradshaw. Little Brown Book Group. 1991.

The Inner Child. Cathryn Taylor. Jeremy P Tarcher (Penguin Group USA). 1991.

Recovery of Your Inner Child. Lucia Capacchione. Simon and Schuster. 1991.

Windswept and Interesting. Billy Connolly. (p247). Two Roads. 2021.

Alcoholics Anonymous (Third Edition). BPCC Hazel Books (GB). 1979.

For your notes:

For your notes:

For your notes: